TITO PUENTE
Mambo King ♔ Rey del Mambo

A **bilingual** picture book by Monica Brown

Illustrated by Rafael López

Translated by Adriana Domínguez

Quill Tree Books
An Imprint of HarperCollinsPublishers

Quill Tree Books is an imprint of HarperCollins Publishers.
HarperCollins Español is an imprint of HarperCollins Publishers.

Tito Puente: Mambo King / Rey del Mambo. Text copyright © 2013 by Monica Brown
Illustrations copyright © 2013 by Rafael López
Translation copyright © 2013 by HarperCollins Publishers
All rights reserved. Manufactured in Italy.
No part of this book may be used or reproduced in any manner whatsoever
without written permission except in the case of brief quotations
embodied in critical articles and reviews. For information address
HarperCollins Children's Books, a division of HarperCollins Publishers,
195 Broadway, New York, NY 10007. www.harpercollinschildrens.com

Library of Congress Control Number: 2012025493
ISBN 978-0-06-122784-4

The artist used acrylic paint that comes in recycled salsa jars from Mexico
and Liquitex on distressed, hand-cut, and sanded wooden boards
for the illustrations in this book.
Typography by Sarah Hoy and Dana Fritts
24 25 26 27 28 RTLO 10 9 8 7 6 5 4 3 2 1
First paperback edition, 2024

Special thanks to Professor Steven Hemphill from
the music department at Northern Arizona University

Ladies and gentlemen,
boys and girls, clap your hands for Tito Puente. . . .
The Mambo King plays and sways as people dance
the mambo, the rumba, and the cha-cha!

Damas y caballeros,

*niños y niñas, ¡aplaudan a Tito Puente...! ¡El Rey
del Mambo toca su música y se balancea mientras
la audiencia baila el mambo, la rumba y el
chachachá!*

¡Tum Tica!
¡Tac Tic!
¡Tum Tic!
¡Tom Tom!

Before he could walk, Tito was making music. He banged spoons and forks on pots and pans, windowsills and cans.

Aún antes de caminar, Tito ya hacía música. Usaba cucharas y tenedores para golpear ollas y sartenes, alféizares y latas.

¡Tum Tica!
¡Tac Tic!
¡Tum Tic!
¡Tom Tom!

He was so loud his neighbors in Spanish Harlem said, "Get that boy some music lessons!" And that is exactly what his mother did.

Hacía tanto ruido que sus vecinos de El Barrio de Harlem decían:
—¡Lleven a ese niño a tomar clases de música!
Y eso es exactamente lo que hizo su mamá.

Tito loved to dance, too!

¡A Tito también le encantaba bailar!

Every year his church held a Stars of the Future contest.

Little Tito danced and spun and tapped and drummed and . . .

Tito won! He was named King of the Stars. Over the years, Tito became King four times!

◎

Cada año, su iglesia auspiciaba un concurso llamado "Las estrellas del futuro".

El pequeño Tito bailó, giró, zapateó, tamborileó y...

¡Tito ganó! Lo coronaron Rey de las Estrellas. Al paso de los años, ¡Tito fue nombrado rey cuatro veces!

¡Bam!

¡Slam!

When he wasn't playing music, Tito played baseball with sticks on the streets of his neighborhood.

Cuando no estaba tocando música, Tito jugaba al béisbol con palos de madera en las calles de su barrio.

Tito performed at parties, restaurants, and clubs. His first band was called Los Happy Boys, and their music made people happy.

✳

Tito tocaba en fiestas, restaurantes y clubes nocturnos. Su primera banda se llamaba Los Happy Boys. Su música hacía que la gente se sintiera feliz.

During World War II, Tito was in the Navy. He joined the ship's band and learned to play the saxophone and write music. After the war, Tito went to the Juilliard School of Music and dreamed of having his own band.

Tito formó parte de la Marina durante la Segunda Guerra Mundial. Allí se unió a la banda de su barco y aprendió a tocar el saxófono y a escribir música. Después de la guerra, Tito estudió en la Escuela de Música Juilliard. Soñaba con tener su propia orquesta.

On weekends Tito played magical mambos and beautiful cha-chas with different bands at the Palladium Ballroom in New York City. People loved dancing to salsa and the rhythms of Tito and his timbales. Still, he wished he could be the bandleader.

Durante los fines de semana, Tito tocaba mambos mágicos y chachachás bellos con diferentes bandas en el salón de baile Palladium, en Nueva York. A la audiencia le encantaba bailar al son de la salsa y de los diferentes ritmos que Tito tocaba con sus timbales. Sin embargo, él seguía deseando ser director de una orquesta.

Tito's dream finally came true when he led his very own big band—the Tito Puente Orchestra. He wrote music and recorded more than one hundred albums! He made music with Celia Cruz, Santana, and La Lupe.

El sueño de Tito al fin se hizo realidad cuando logró dirigir su propia orquesta: la Orquesta de Tito Puente. ¡Tito escribió su propia música y grabó más de cien álbumes! Hizo música con Celia Cruz, Santana y La Lupe.

When the Tito Puente Orchestra played . . .
the tambourines sounded like rain on
metal roofs.

Cuando la Orquesta de Tito Puente
tocaba . . . las panderetas sonaban como
la lluvia cayendo sobre techos de metal.

The horns blew high and loud
and strong and low.

Los cuernos soplaban altos y
agudos, fuertes y graves.

The claves smacked clackity clackity clack clack,
and everyone's feet went tappity tap.
Best of all, Tito played the timbales . . .

Las claves se golpeaban cláquiti, cláquiti, clac,
clac y todos los pies hacían tápiti, tap.
Y lo mejor de todo, Tito tocaba sus timbales...

¡Tum Tica!
¡Tac Tic!
¡Tum Tic!
¡Tom Tom!

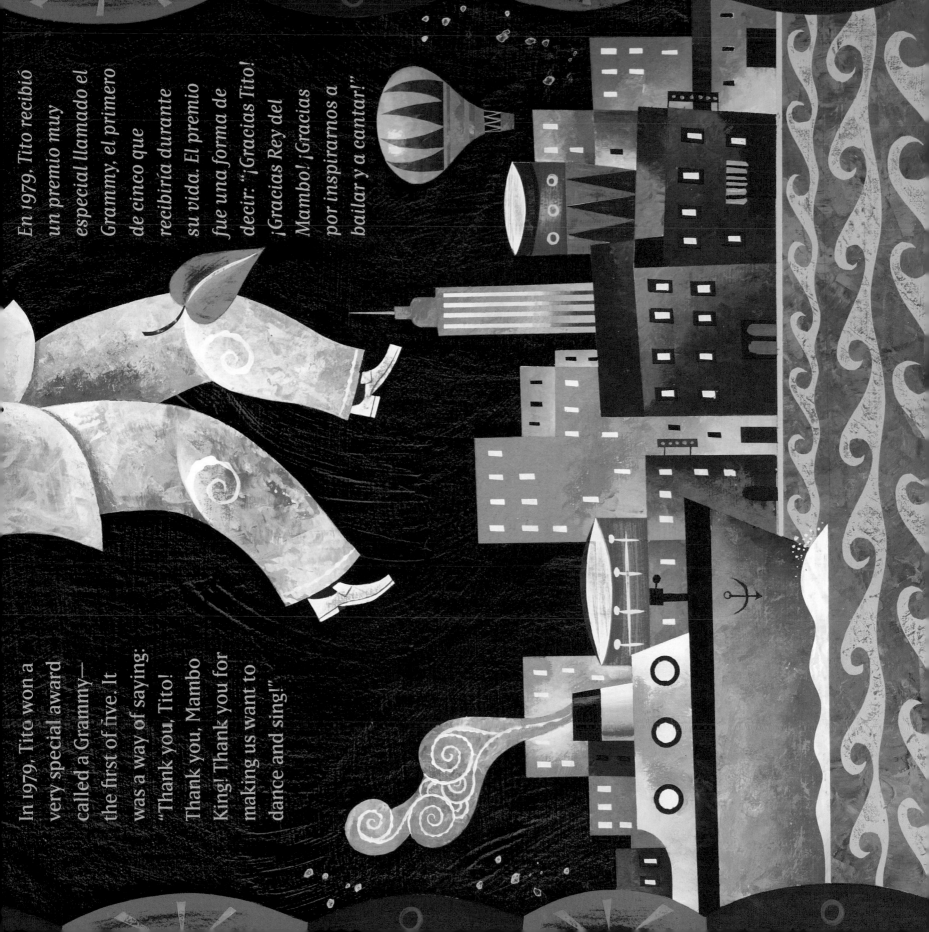

En 1979, Tito recibió un premio muy especial llamado el Grammy, el primero de cinco que recibiría durante su vida. El premio fue una forma de decir: "¡Gracias Tito! ¡Gracias Rey del Mambo! ¡Gracias por inspirarnos a bailar y a cantar!"

In 1979, Tito won a very special award called a Grammy— the first of five. It was a way of saying: "Thank you, Tito! Thank you, Mambo King! Thank you for making us want to dance and sing!"

¡Tum

Tica!

The dancers twirled, the lights swirled, and the mambo went on and on. . . .

Los bailarines giraban, las luces daban vueltas en espiral y el mambo seguía y seguía...

¡Tac Tic!

¡Tum Tic!

TITO PUENTE
Biography
(April 20, 1923–June 1, 2000)

*E*rnest Anthony Puente Jr. was born at Harlem Hospital in New York City in 1923. Everyone in Spanish Harlem called him Ernestito, or Tito for short.

Not only was Tito Puente considered the "King of the Mambo" and the "Godfather of Salsa," but he was at the center of the Latin jazz explosion. His musical career spanned half a century and crossed both musical and national borders.

During his lifetime, Tito Puente recorded 118 albums and won five Grammies, including the Grammy Lifetime Achievement Award. He collaborated with the most famous Latin musicians of the twentieth century, including Machito, Santana, Willie Bobo, Gloria Estefan, La Lupe, and especially Celia Cruz. Tito founded the Tito Puente Educational Foundation, which offers scholarships to students to study music at the Juilliard School of Music. He wanted to inspire other young musicians to pursue their dreams.